vjbnf
025.6 LOVE

Lovett, Amber, author
A better library checkout
33410015435615      08/01/19

DISCARDED
Valparaiso-Porter County
Library System

Valparaiso Public Library
103 Jefferson Street
Valparaiso, IN 46383

21ST Century Skills **INNOVATION LIBRARY** | Design a Better World

# A Better Library Checkout

Amber Lovett

Published in the United States of America by Cherry Lake Publishing
Ann Arbor, Michigan
www.cherrylakepublishing.com

Content Adviser: Kristin Fontichiaro, University of Michigan School of Information, Ann Arbor, MI
Reading Adviser: Marla Conn MS, Ed., Literacy specialist, Read-Ability, Inc.

Photo Credits: © NuMameaw7438/Shutterstock.com, cover, 1; © New Africa/Shutterstock.com, 5; © Syda Productions/Shutterstock.com, 6; © StockSnap/pixabay.com, 9; © GaudiLab/Shutterstock.com, 10; © chalermphon_tiam/Shutterstock.com, 15; © Anna Berdnik/Shutterstock.com, 17; © Oleksii Didok/Shutterstock.com, 19; © wavebreakmedia/Shutterstock.com, 29

Graphic Element Credits: © Ohn Mar/Shutterstock.com, back cover, multiple interior pages; © Dmitrieva Katerina/Shutterstock.com, back cover, multiple interior pages; © advent/Shutterstock.com, back cover, front cover, multiple interior pages; © Visual Generation/Shutterstock.com, multiple interior pages; © anfisa focusova/Shutterstock.com, front cover, multiple interior pages; © Babich Alexander/Shutterstock.com, back cover, front cover, multiple interior pages

Copyright © 2019 by Cherry Lake Publishing

All rights reserved. No part of this book may be reproduced or utilized
in any form or by any means without written permission from the publisher.

Library of Congress Cataloging-in-Publication Data

Names: Lovett, Amber, author.
Title: A better library checkout / by Amber Lovett.
Description: Ann Arbor : Cherry Lake Publishing, [2019] | Series: Design a
  better world | Includes bibliographical references and index.
Identifiers: LCCN 2018037690| ISBN 9781534143227 (hardcover) | ISBN
  9781534139787 (pbk.) | ISBN 9781534140981 (pdf) | ISBN 9781534142183
  (hosted ebook)
Subjects: LCSH: School libraries—Circulation and loans—Juvenile literature.
Classification: LCC Z675.S3 L87 2019 | DDC 025.6—dc23
LC record available at https://lccn.loc.gov/2018037690

Printed in the United States of America
Corporate Graphics

# Table of Contents

**Chapter One**
Design Thinking and Identifying a Problem ......... 4

**Chapter Two**
Research, Interview, and Observe ......... 8

**Chapter Three**
Synthesize and Focus ......... 14

**Chapter Four**
Brainstorm ......... 18

**Chapter Five**
Prototype ......... 22

**Chapter Six**
Test, Adjust, Test Again ......... 24

**Chapter Seven**
Implement! ......... 28

Learn More ......... 30
Glossary ......... 31
Index ......... 32

## CHAPTER ONE

# Design Thinking and Identifying a Problem

Have you ever stood in a long line and wondered if there was a way to make it move faster? Or maybe you've thought about how your favorite app would be more enjoyable with one small change. Perhaps you wish you could make something you use all the time—like your water bottle or lunch box—a little bit better. When you find something that could use improvement, this is called a **design problem**.

You may wonder why people have not invented solutions to these problems. Instead of wondering, why not design a solution yourself? You might just create something that can help make the lives of friends and family a little bit easier.

If you don't know where to start, don't worry. You can use a process called **design thinking** to help you. Design thinking helps you solve a problem by following steps to understand the problem and come up with ideas for a solution. Design thinking was started by a company called IDEO in California. People have used design thinking to solve all kinds of problems, like how to open a car door when your hands are full or how to

Design thinking helps you look at ordinary objects—like toothbrushes!—and think of ways to make them better.

...... slick is a good example of an innovation that solved an everyday problem.

make brushing your teeth more comfortable. All kinds of people and companies use design thinking to create solutions to everyday problems.

This book is designed to help you explore the design thinking process by coming up with ideas for improving the way your library checks out books. In each chapter, we'll explore a step in the process so that you can find a way to make your library better!

## Try This

Visit your local library. This could be your school's library or a public library. Bring a notebook with you. Then, find a book to check out. You may have to go up to the librarian to check out the book. Or the library might offer **self-checkout** with a **bar code** scanner set up for people to use. Make notes about any problems you encounter. Is there anything frustrating or difficult to understand? What is good or bad about your experience? Take note of these things and any possible design problems. You'll use that list to guide your work in Chapter 2.

## CHAPTER TWO

# Research, Interview, and Observe

Now that you have an idea of the problem you want to solve, it's time to find out what other people think. In design thinking, you can interview other people, **observe**, and do research to help you solve your design problem.

## Research

Doing research online can help you learn more about how libraries work. A Google image search using keywords like "public library checkout" or "school library checkout" can help you see examples of how different libraries organize their checkout **systems**. Try using the word *circulation* in your search, too, instead of *checkout*, because that is the formal term used in libraries. You can also visit the website for your library, if it has one. You may discover that these libraries have a site that lists all the books the library owns, called a **catalog**. The catalog is what librarians use to help them keep track of where their books are located and who has checked them out. Looking at the catalog can give you a lot of useful information about your library.

Try walking through the library with a friend as they borrow a book. How do they interact with the checkout system?

Talk to friends, teachers, and other library patrons about what they like and dislike about their library.

Here are some notes we made during our online research:
- Some libraries have more than one desk where librarians sit.
- Sometimes librarians check out books, and sometimes there is a self-checkout system.
- Some libraries have big signs that show you where to check out books, but some do not.

## Interview

Asking questions is a great way to find out the problems that other people have using the library. If your problem is at the school's library, ask your classmates and teachers. If your problem is at the public library, you can ask your friends and family members. No matter what library, you can talk to the librarians who work there. Come up with a list of questions to ask that will get people to tell you what they like and dislike about checking out books. Be sure to use open-ended questions. For example:

- Can you tell me about how you find and check out books?
- How long does it take you to check out your books? Do you have enough time to check them out?
- How do you feel when you visit the library? Why?
- Have you ever felt frustrated while checking out books? Why?
- Is there anything confusing about checking out books?
- If there were one thing you could change about the library, what would it be?
- What is your least favorite part of visiting (or working at) the library? What is your favorite part?

You may want to make a list of questions in your notebook. Skip a few lines under each question so you have space to make notes. You can make a new printout or copy of the page and ask the same questions to everyone you interview.

## Observe

Observation is a great way to find solutions to problems. To be a good observer, you need to look carefully. Watch what people do and ask yourself, *why* are they doing that?

Visit your library again. Observe the people checking out books. What do you notice? Is there a line to check out books? Are there people waiting who need help? Are students able to find books to check out, and do they know how to check them out? Can everyone reach the counter easily, or do they need to use something like a stool? Do people who use a wheelchair have a good checkout experience? Notice if people look happy, upset, bored, or confused while checking out books.

Examples of observations you might make:
- There is only one line, and people are always waiting.
- Lines are the longest 5 minutes before the end of the library checkout time.
- Students spend most of their library time finding books.
- Six students ran out of time and could not check out their books.

## Notes, Sketches, and Photos

It's very important that you take notes to help you keep track of your observations, research, and the information you get from other people. These are not like notes for class. You do not need complete sentences. Just write the most important words that will help you remember your thoughts later. Your notes can also include sketches and photos. Visual references will help you remember exactly what you saw.

# Try This

1. **Research:** Do a Google Image search for library check-outs. Browse some of the findings. What do you see that is different from your library? What things seem useful?
2. **Interview:** Conduct at least two interviews with typical users and one with a librarian. The librarian will have a different point of view since he or she works in the library all day and knows the most about the library.
3. **Observe:** Go to the library during different times of day (you may need to ask your teacher for permission to do this during class time). Make notes about what you see during different times of day or with different classes that use the library.

# CHAPTER THREE

# Synthesize and Focus

Now it is time to **synthesize**, which means looking at the big picture your notes create, and **focus** on the problem you want to solve.

## Synthesize

First, lay out all your notes on a table. You may want to read them aloud. Grab a friend or family member to help you. This will make it more fun, and they may see things you miss. As you read your notes, look for **patterns**. Notice the ideas that come up more than once. Write down any patterns you notice. For example, you may notice that more than one of the people you talked with complained about waiting in line for a long time, and you also observed people standing in long lines. This is a pattern that you can write down.

Here are some of the patterns we observed in our library:

- Students did not know how to find books they wanted.
- Students were afraid to ask the librarian questions.
- The librarian was too busy checking out books to answer questions right after school.

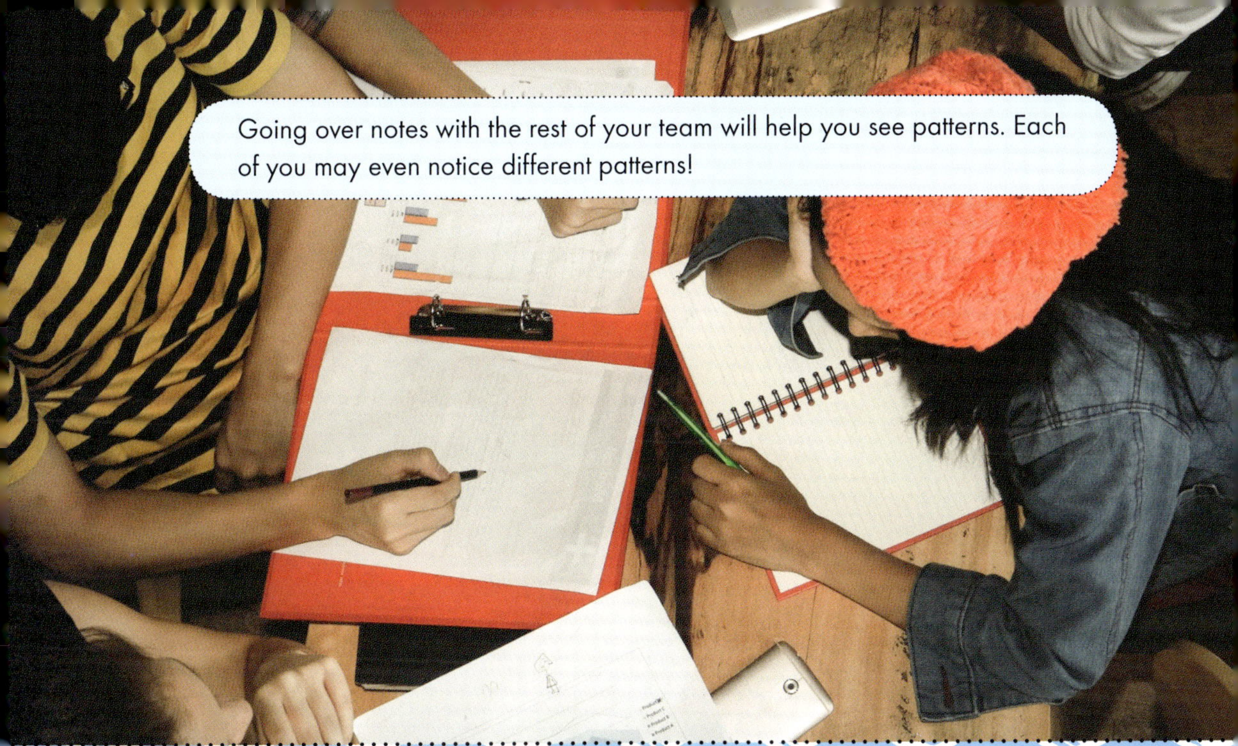

Going over notes with the rest of your team will help you see patterns. Each of you may even notice different patterns!

## Try This

Look over your notes with your friends. Make a list of the patterns you find. Now choose one problem that we'll use in the next chapter.

- Students did not have enough time to find and check out books during lunchtime.
- Students didn't want to wait to check out books, so they left the library.

## Focus

The patterns you notice can help you focus on the problem you want to solve. Pick the one that you think is the most important or exciting to you. For now, don't worry about solving the problem. You just need to decide which problem you want to solve so you are ready for the next step!

Using sticky notes is a good way to record ideas and look at patterns. Use a different color for each different theme.

## CHAPTER FOUR

# Brainstorm

Now that you have picked a problem, you might have a solution already in your head. Before you rush off to try and test it, you still need to think about other solutions. Sometimes, our first idea is not our best idea. That's why we **brainstorm** to come up with as many ideas as possible *before* we build a prototype. Set a timer for 5 minutes and try to come up with as many ideas as you can in that time. Write each idea down on a separate sticky note. It's even better to do this with some friends!

To help you think of ideas, ask yourself, "To solve _____, we will design and test *what*?" When we tried this, we said, To solve students leaving the library because lines are too long, we will try:

- Requiring students to get in line to check out their books 5 minutes before class ends
- Adding a self-checkout computer and scanner
- Letting students check out books on a paper sign-out sheet
- Getting the librarian a helper during busy times
- Giving students a special time when their class can come to check out books

Brainstorming solutions should be creative—and fun! For the best results, everyone should agree to listen and not interrupt.

- Moving the bar codes on the books so they are easier to scan
- Setting up a computer so students can find books more easily and have more time to check them out
- Finding a way to check out books without scanning them
- Not allowing students to check out books for 10 minutes after school
- Reserving the first 10 minutes after school for asking questions of the librarian, not checking out books
- Creating a book delivery system to send books to students' classes
- Labeling the books and creating signs so it is easier to find popular series or topics

You may notice that some of these solutions involve designing a new kind of product, and some involve making a new system or way of doing things. The great thing about design thinking is that it helps you find solutions you may never have thought of before. This is why we brainstorm. You might find there is an easy change that could make a big difference!

We decided that we would try the solution of letting students check out books on a paper sign-out sheet.

## Try This

Get a stack of sticky notes and some friends. Read them the pattern you picked in Chapter 3 and say, "To solve _____, we will design and test *what*?" Set the timer and ask each group member to work silently to put one solution on each sticky note. When the timer goes off, arrange the sticky notes randomly on a wall or table. One person can read the ideas aloud. If you have trouble deciding which idea is best, have everyone walk around the table and put a dot on two to three ideas that they think are best. Then, count the votes and find out what your top solution is. Keep the other ideas safe, in case you want to look back at them later!

# CHAPTER FIVE

# Prototype

By now, you should have a good idea of the solution you want to create. The next step is to create a **prototype** of your solution. A prototype is like a first draft. It does not have to be perfect. In fact, it shouldn't be! Depending on the solution you have decided on, you may choose to make a prototype in a number of ways. If you have a product you want to design, you can use cheap building materials like paper, cardboard, clay, or fabric to build a model of it. Since we decided to test a paper sign-out system, or log, all we needed was a sheet of paper and a pencil to create a draft of what it might look like.

The best prototypes don't need to take a long time to create, and they don't need to be beautiful. Their only purpose is to help show your idea to others, so they can understand what you are trying to create. Don't worry if your prototype isn't perfect. The next step will help you find the flaws in your design so your finished product will be even better.

## Try This

First, think about your solution. What would be the best way to show others how it would work? If you need to, gather materials to build a model of your idea. You should be able to find almost everything you need to build a prototype in your own home. Look for recycled materials, paper, scissors, tape, LEGO bricks, or whatever else you have handy.

If you are not designing a product, then you might want to draw a sketch of your idea. This works great if you are thinking of designing an app or website for your solution. If your prototype is a new system for how to do things, then you could write down the steps for the new process so you are ready to test it in the next chapter.

## CHAPTER SIX

# Test, Adjust, Test Again

Now that you have a prototype of your idea, it is time for one of the most important steps in design thinking: testing. You may have wondered why you built a prototype instead of just building a solution. The reason is that inventing things can cost you a lot of time and money, so it is better to test them *before* you create a finished product. Imagine if your favorite smartphone company sent you a cell phone without testing it first. The buttons might stop working, it might be too slippery to hold, or the battery might not last long enough. Companies test their products to get them just right so that these things don't happen. Now you have a chance to test your solution too.

## Testing Your Invention with Users

Testing your invention can be a lot of fun, but it can also be tricky. You might think that your solution is perfect as it is! But sometimes it can be hard to see our own mistakes. Remember that listening to what others have to say does not mean your idea is bad—it means it is still a rough draft. Every idea can use a little improvement.

The first thing you need to do is find some people to test your prototype. You might want to ask your librarian and some friends who use your library for their feedback. First, explain the problem you are trying to solve. Then, explain what your prototype is and how you think it will solve the problem. Make sure everyone understands that your prototype is just a rough draft. Ask them for feedback that can help you make your idea better.

If you are nervous about hearing other people's feedback, then have them fill out a worksheet of questions that you can read later. You can use the sentences here to make sure your friends give you helpful feedback without hurting your feelings:

- I like _____ because _____.
- My favorite part of this invention is _____. It would really help _____.
- I wonder if _____ would help you solve the problem too.
- I wonder what would happen if you tried _____.

Make sure you take notes if you ask for feedback in person!

The solution we prototyped was a handout where people could write down their name and the book's bar code. Because this was an easy fix, we actually tried to set up this system in the school library. We made a sign with the directions, put out blank sheets and pencils, and watched what happened. We took notes and asked people for feedback. We asked the school librarian what she thought of the system and the extra time it took her at the end of the day to type in the bar codes by hand.

## Reviewing Feedback

Read over the notes that your users made. As you read, remember to think about your original problem. Ask yourself if each idea would make your solution better. Do the new ideas help you solve the problem? You don't have to listen to an idea if it will not help solve the problem.

In our situation, we got feedback like this:
- Paper log took a lot of time to fill out.
- Add a picture so students know what the bar code number looks like.
- I'm not sure what the bar code number is.
- Make it an online form.
- Some students have messy handwriting.
- Some students did not fill out the whole form.

## Adjust and Test Again

Now that you have your feedback, you can change your prototype. You might only need to make a small change, or the ideas from your friends might inspire you to start over with a new and improved prototype.

With our feedback, we noticed that more than one person was worried about handwriting and missing information. The idea for an online form could help solve these problems. We could also put a picture of what the bar code number looks like on the online form.

We decided to test a new prototype for an online Google Form, and we got much better feedback from our users! The librarian really liked being able to cut and paste numbers from the form into the circulation software. She said it was much more accurate than typing in the bar code numbers.

## Try This

Find some friends and show them your prototype. Explain your idea and ask for helpful feedback (in person or through a paper or online survey). Read over their ideas and improve your prototype, or make a new one. Now, test it again and see what your friends think!

## CHAPTER SEVEN

# Implement!

Now that you have improved your prototype, it's time to create your final product.

Depending on what your solution is, you might need help from a trusted adult to purchase supplies and build your product. If you are designing a system like our online checkout form, then you probably need to talk to your librarian and ask if he or she will try out your solution in the library.

Even if you aren't able to create a "real" final product, you can still show your ideas to your classmates, teacher, and librarian. Try making a poster or video about your idea to show others your hard work. Or send a letter to the company that makes the library's circulation software to let them know your solution is a tested and successful idea.

You should be proud! You have made it through the design thinking process and have learned about how inventors come up with new ideas. Think about all the ways that you can use this process to solve other everyday problems—and keep inventing!

## Try This

Ask your librarian to look at your final prototype. Explain how you think your idea can help the library. Your librarian might even decide to try your idea!

# Learn More

## Books

Beattie, Rob. *Invent It! Turn Your Small Idea into the World's Next Great Invention!* New York: Sterling, 2017.

Fontichiaro, Kristin. *Design Thinking*. Ann Arbor, MI: Cherry Lake Publishing, 2015.

## Websites

**Kids Think Design**
www.kidsthinkdesign.org/index.html
Learn more about different kinds of designers and test your skills with design challenges.

**PBS Kids—Design Squad Global**
http://pbskids.org/designsquad
This website has challenges and games to help you improve your design skills.

# Glossary

**bar code** (BAR KODE) thick and thin black lines that computers can read to get information about a book

**brainstorm** (BRAYN-storm) to think of as many ideas as possible

**catalog** (KAT-uh-lawg) a system that stores the information about all the books that a library owns

**circulation** (sur-kyuh-LAY-shuhn) a library term for checking out items

**design problem** (dih-ZINE PRAH-bluhm) something that doesn't work well that you think you can make better

**design thinking** (dih-ZINE THINGK-ing) a process for studying, testing, and solving problems

**feedback** (FEED-bak) information you get back after doing or saying something

**focus** (FOH-kuhs) to narrow down to one idea or really concentrate on one thing

**observe** (uhb-ZURV) to look closely at something

**patterns** (PAT-urnz) when the same thing or similar thing shows up more than once

**prototype** (PROH-tuh-tipe) a "first draft" of an invention

**self-checkout** (SELF CHEK-out) a system that lets someone borrow library books without asking the librarian

**synthesize** (SIN-thuh-size) to look at a lot of ideas and figure out what the big picture is or what the patterns are

**systems** (SIS-tumz) organized ways of getting things done

# Index

brainstorming, 18–21

design problem, 4, 10, 16
design team
    brainstorming, 18–21
    synthesizing information, 15
design thinking, 4–7, 20, 24

feedback, 25–27
final product, 24, 28
focus, 14, 16

ideas
    brainstorming, 18–21
    implementation, 28
    prototyping, 22–23
    synthesizing, 14–17
    testing, 24–27
IDEO, 4
implementation, 28
interviews, 8, 10–11, 13
    synthesizing, 14–17

library check out system, 6, 7

notes, 7, 10, 12
    synthesizing, 14–17

observation, 8, 11–12, 13
    synthesizing, 14–17

patterns, 14, 15, 16, 17
photos, 12
problem identification, 4–7
prototype, 22–23
    feedback, 25–27
    implementation, 28
    testing, 24–27

research, 8–10, 13
    synthesizing, 14–17

sketches, 12, 23
solution, 4, 6, 11
    brainstorming, 18–21
    implementation, 28
    prototyping, 22–23
    testing, 24–27
sticky notes, 17, 18, 21
synthesizing, 14–17

testing, 24–27
themes, 17

users, 13, 24–26

**Amber Lovett** is a librarian at Salpointe Catholic High School in Tucson, Arizona. She is the author of four maker books for kids.